Great
Jewish
Quotes

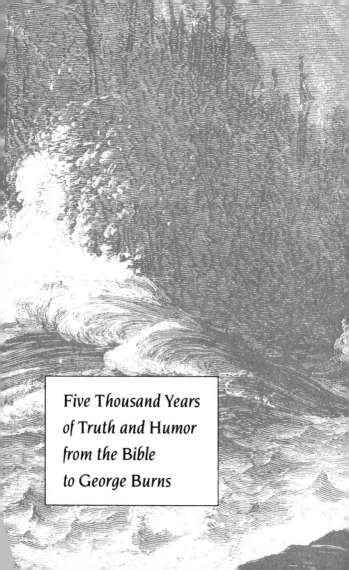

Five Thousand Years
of Truth and Humor
from the Bible
to George Burns

Great Jewish Quotes

Noah benShea

Ballantine Books · New York

Copyright © 1993 by Noah benShea

All rights reserved under International and Pan-
American Copyright Conventions. Published in the
United States by Ballantine Books, a division of
Random House, Inc., New York, and simultaneously in
Canada by Random House of Canada Limited, Toronto.

Library of Congress Catalog Card Number: 93-90804
ISBN: 0-345-38345-1

Cover design by Judy Herbstman
Text design by Beth Tondreau Design / Mary A. Wirth

Manufactured in the United States of America
First Edition: November 1993

10 9 8 7 6 5 4 3 2 1

For *my brothers*
LORNE and NEIL

Thank you
to my editors,
Joëlle Delbourgo and Virginia Faber,
for inviting me into the experience
of writing this book
and
to my wife,
Danyel benShea,
for her invaluable patience
and discriminating wit

In the Beginning . . .

While putting this book together I have often felt like a man walking in a shower of wisdom, each drop wet with its own insight.

The criteria for inclusion, other than the author's preference, is if the quotes are: part of the religious tradition, for example, the Old Testament or the Talmud, the folk tradition, tales and Yiddish sources, or attributed to noteworthy Jewish voices over time.

May I suggest that these layers of thought, ranging from the ancient and pious to the modern and cynical, be treated like a box of the finest chocolates. Taken one at a time, the sweetness will linger.

Lastly, a word about whose book this is. As we are each the source of the other's river, my hope is that in this book of *Great Jewish Quotes* you will find currents of truth, streams of compassion, and rivers of humor on which you may float a ride to your own soul's source.

—Noah benShea, 1993

Good deeds
are better
than wise sayings.

—TALMUD: PIRKE AVOT

People think all I have to do is stand up
and tell a few jokes.
Well, that's not as easy as it looks.
Every year it gets to be more of an
effort to stand up.

—GEORGE BURNS

Great Jewish Quotes

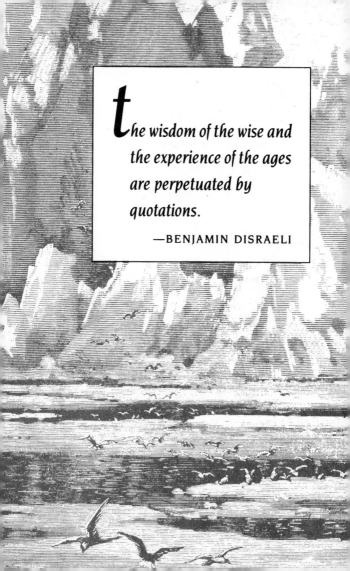

*t*he wisdom of the wise and
the experience of the ages
are perpetuated by
quotations.

—BENJAMIN DISRAELI

*O*ne should accept the
truth from whatever
source it proceeds.

—MAIMONIDES

*g*od casts the die,
not the dice.

—ALBERT EINSTEIN

*e*xperience is what we call
the accumulation of our
mistakes.

—YIDDISH FOLK SAYING

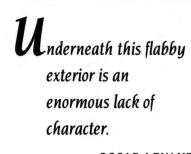

*U*nderneath this flabby exterior is an enormous lack of character.

—OSCAR LEVANT

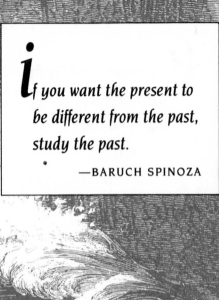

*i*f you want the present to
be different from the past,
study the past.

—BARUCH SPINOZA

*i*f you want to give God a good laugh, tell him your plans.

—YIDDISH FOLK SAYING

i do not believe in God
I believe in cashmere.

—FRAN LEBOWITZ

i talk to myself because I like dealing with a better class of people.

—JACKIE MASON

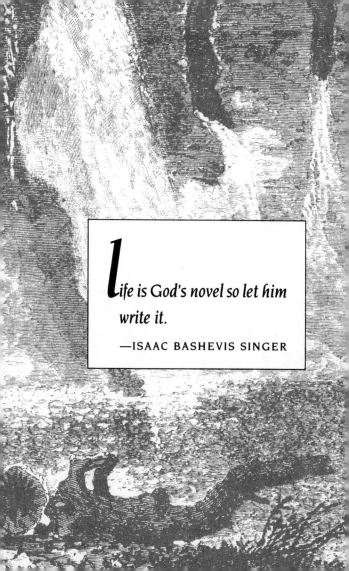

*l*ife is God's novel so let him write it.

—ISAAC BASHEVIS SINGER

*i*ntegrity simply means a willingness not to violate one's identity.

—ERICH FROMM

a salesman is got to dream, boy. It comes with the territory.

—ARTHUR MILLER

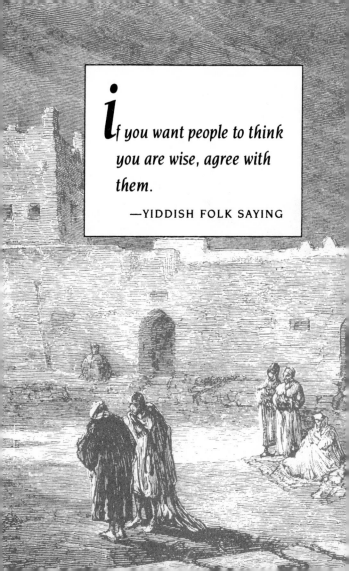

*i*f you want people to think
you are wise, agree with
them.

—YIDDISH FOLK SAYING

*S*anity is a cozy lie.

—SUSAN SONTAG

*C*ompeting pressures tempt one to believe that an issue deferred is a problem avoided; more often it is a crisis invented.

—HENRY KISSINGER

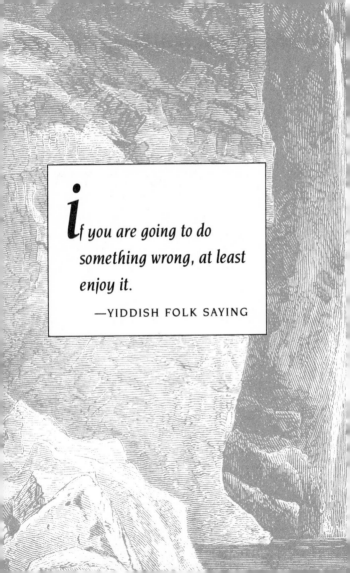

*i*f you are going to do
something wrong, at least
enjoy it.

—YIDDISH FOLK SAYING

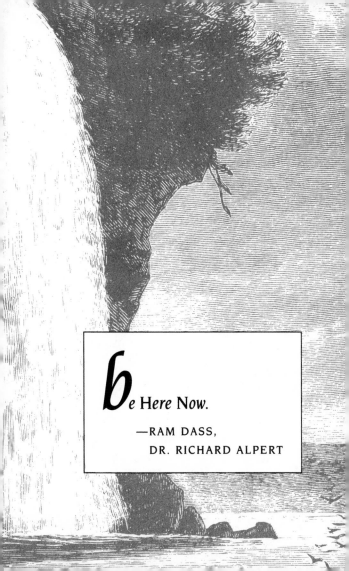

be Here Now.

—RAM DASS,
DR. RICHARD ALPERT

*O*beying from love is better than to obey from fear.

—RASHI,
RABBI SOLOMON BEN ISAAC

a man is only as good as what he loves.

—SAUL BELLOW

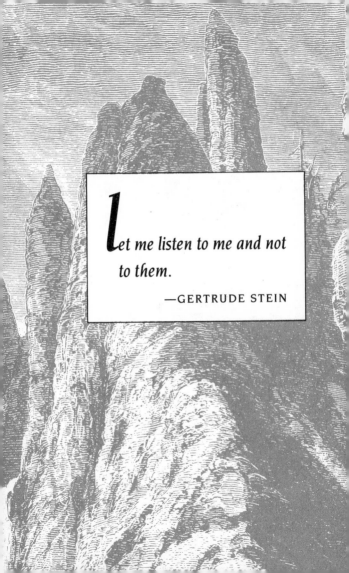

*l*et me listen to me and not to them.

—GERTRUDE STEIN

*t*he best index to a person's character is

(a) how he treats people who can't do him any good, and

(b) how he treats people who can't fight back.

—ABIGAIL VAN BUREN, "DEAR ABBEY"

*W*hat you do not want
others to do to you,
do not do to them.

—RABBI HILLEL,
  TALMUD: PIRKE AVOT

*d*on't threaten a child:
Either punish him or
forgive him.

—TALMUD

*i*nsanity is hereditary;
you can get it from your
children.

—SAM LEVENSON

*W*e are generally more convinced by the reasons we discover on our own than by those given to us by others.

—MARCEL PROUST

*t*o have a friend be one.

—VISCOUNT
SAMUEL HERBERT

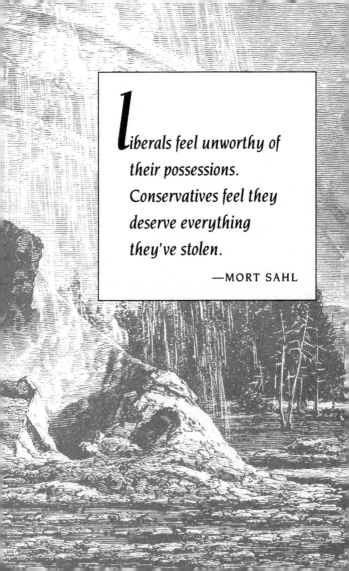

*L*iberals feel unworthy of
their possessions.
Conservatives feel they
deserve everything
they've stolen.

—MORT SAHL

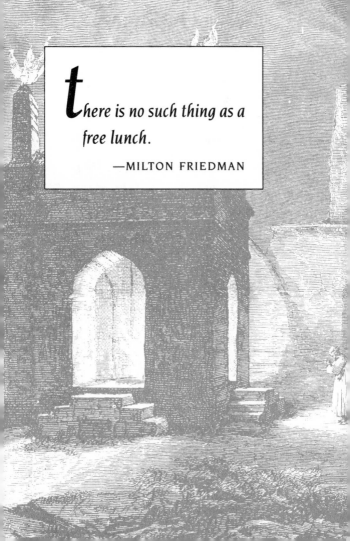

*t*here is no such thing as a free lunch.

—MILTON FRIEDMAN

*t*hose who submerge
themselves in the desire
for money are always
in debt.

—RABBI NAHMAN BEN SIMHA,
THE BRATSLAVER

$y$ou don't have to be big
to be great.

—SHALOM ALEICHEM

*O*ne who desires the attention of others has not yet found himself.

—RAV SHLOMO WOLBE

*S*urrounding yourself with dwarfs does not make you a giant.

—YIDDISH FOLK SAYING

*t*he first focus in life here
on earth is to be at peace
with all men.

—RABBI JOEL BEN
ABRAHAM SHEMARIAH

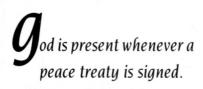

*g*od is present whenever a peace treaty is signed.

—RABBI NAHMAN BEN SIMHA,
THE BRATSLAVER

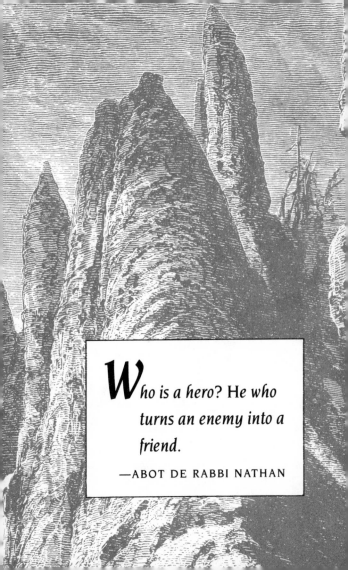

*W*ho is a hero? He who turns an enemy into a friend.

—ABOT DE RABBI NATHAN

*W*e all live with the
objective of being
happy; our lives are all
different and yet the
same.

—ANNE FRANK

*t*wo are better than one,
for if they fall, the one will
lift up his fellow.

—BIBLE, ECCLES. 49:10

i don't think of all the misery, but of all the beauty that still remains.

—ANNE FRANK

*n*ature uses only the longest threads to weave her patterns, so each small piece of her fabric reveals the organization of the entire tapestry.

—RICHARD FEYNMAN

*t*he toughest thing about
  being a success is that
  you've got to keep on
  being a success.

  —IRVING BERLIN

*O*ne thing about being successful is that I stopped being afraid of dying. Once you're a star you're dead already. You're embalmed.

—DUSTIN HOFFMAN

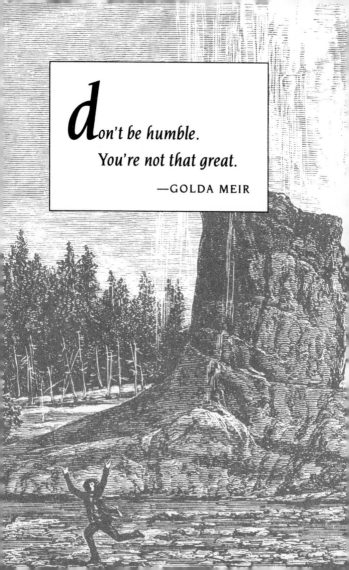

*d*on't be humble.
You're not that great.

—GOLDA MEIR

*W*hether our work is art or science or the daily work of society, it is only the form in which we explore our experience which is different.

—JACOB BRONOWSKI

*Y*ou can fool all the people all the time if the advertising is right and the budget is big enough.

—JOSEPH E. LEVINE

*t*here is only one way to find out if a man is honest—ask him. If he says "yes," you know he's crooked.

—GROUCHO MARX

*t*he secret of the demagogue is to make himself as stupid as his audience so that they can believe they are as clever as he.

—KARL KRAUS

a fool is his own informer.

—YIDDISH FOLK SAYING

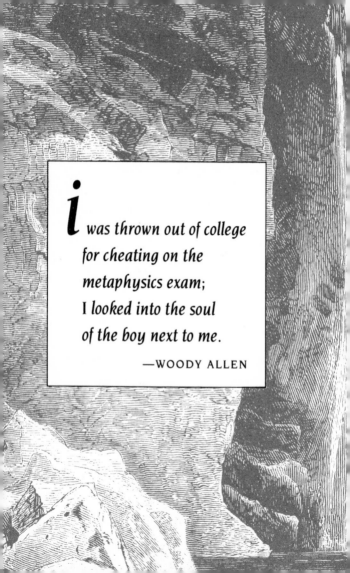

i was thrown out of college
for cheating on the
metaphysics exam;
I looked into the soul
of the boy next to me.

—WOODY ALLEN

*S*cience without religion is
lame, religion without
science is blind.

—ALBERT EINSTEIN

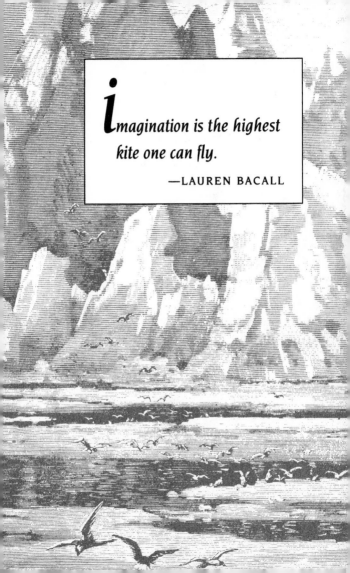

*i*magination is the highest
kite one can fly.

—LAUREN BACALL

*t*ruth rests with God
alone, and a little bit
with me.

—YIDDISH FOLK SAYING

" *f* or example"
is not proof.

—YIDDISH FOLK SAYING

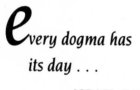

*e*very dogma has
its day . . .

—ISRAEL ZANGWILL

*t*here are children playing
in the streets who could
solve some of my top
problems in physics,
because they have modes
of sensory perception
that I lost long ago.

—J. ROBERT OPPENHEIMER

*t*oo bad that all the people who know how to run the country are busy driving taxicabs and cutting hair.

—GEORGE BURNS

All I know is I'm not
a Marxist.

—KARL MARX

against every great and noble endeavor are a thousand mediocre minds.

—ALBERT EINSTEIN

*t*he establishment is made
up of little men, very
frightened.

—BELLA ABZUG

*e*vil does not prevail until it is given power.

—RABBI EL'AZAR,
THE ZOHAR

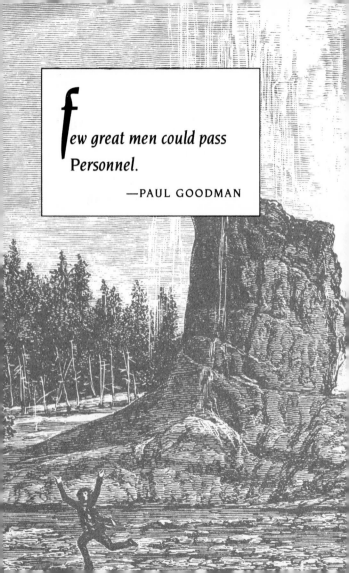

*f*ew great men could pass
Personnel.

—PAUL GOODMAN

***a**nybody who gets out of college having had his confidence in the perfection of existing institutions affirmed has not been educated. Just suffocated.*

—AL CAPP

*t*he meaning of life is that
it stops.

—FRANZ KAFKA

*O*nly our concept of time
makes it possible for us to
speak of the Day of
Judgement by that
name; in reality it is a
constant court in
perpetual session.

—FRANZ KAFKA

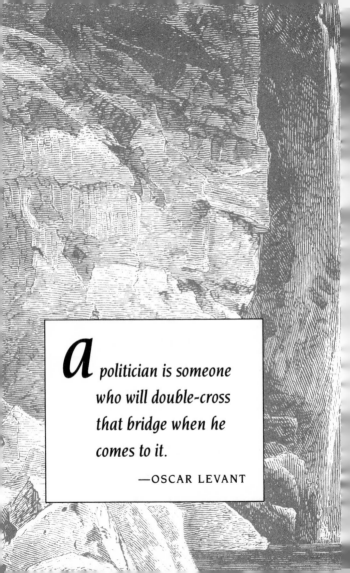

a politician is someone who will double-cross that bridge when he comes to it.

—OSCAR LEVANT

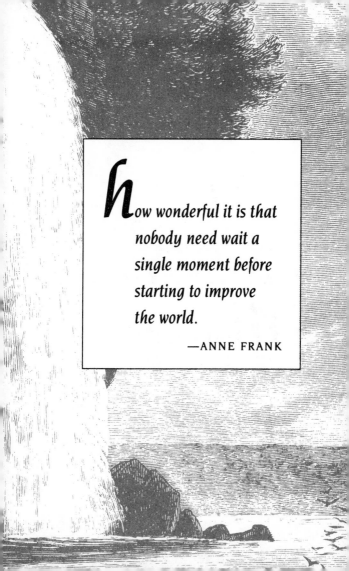

*h*ow wonderful it is that nobody need wait a single moment before starting to improve the world.

—ANNE FRANK

*M*en and nations
behave wisely
once they have
exhausted all the
other alternatives.

—ABBA EBAN

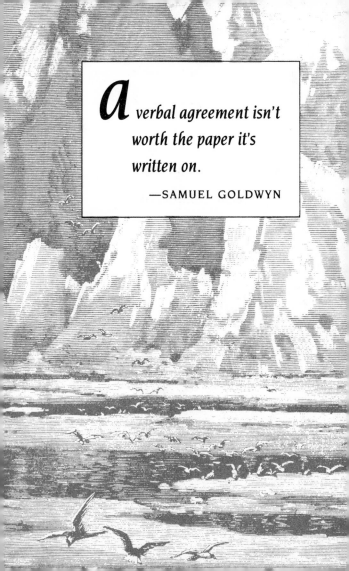

a verbal agreement isn't worth the paper it's written on.

—SAMUEL GOLDWYN

*i*t is easier to fight for one's principles than to live up to them.

—ALFRED ADLER

Speak to the earth, and it
shall teach you.

—BIBLE, JOB 12:8

*N*ext to knowing when to seize an opportunity, the most important thing in life is to know when to forgo an advantage.

—BENJAMIN DISRAELI

*t*he door of success is
marked "push" and
"pull." Achieving success
is knowing when
to do what.

—YIDDISH FOLK SAYING

***M**an is ultimately
self-determining.*

—VIKTOR E. FRANKL

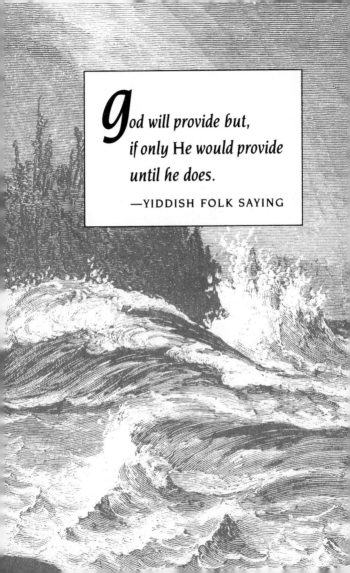

*g*od will provide but,
if only He would provide
until he does.

—YIDDISH FOLK SAYING

*i*f you have money, you are
wise and good-looking and
can sing well too.

—YIDDISH FOLK SAYING

*M*oney doesn't talk,
it swears.

—BOB DYLAN

*t*here is nothing better for
a man than that he
should eat and drink and
make his soul enjoy
pleasure. . . .

—BIBLE, ECCLES. 2:24

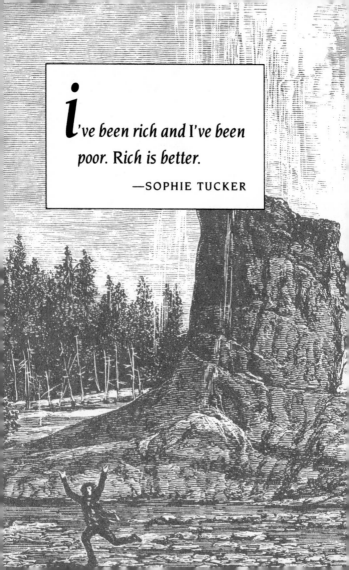

i've been rich and I've been
poor. Rich is better.

—SOPHIE TUCKER

*e*ach social class has its own pathology.

—MARCEL PROUST

*f*ashions in sin change.

—LILLIAN HELLMAN

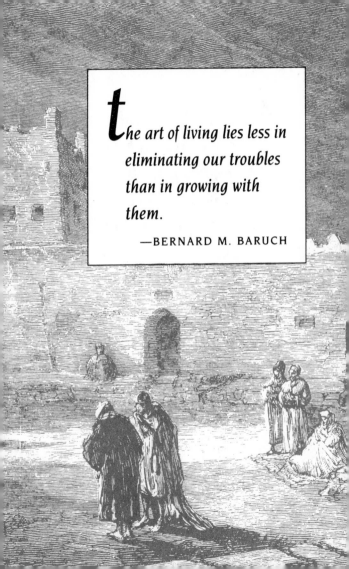

*t*he art of living lies less in
eliminating our troubles
than in growing with
them.

—BERNARD M. BARUCH

a happy woman is one
who has no cares at all;
a cheerful woman is
one who has cares but
doesn't let them get her
down.

—BEVERLY SILLS

*S*trength is not the absence of weakness but how we wrestle with our weaknesses.

—NOAH BENSHEA

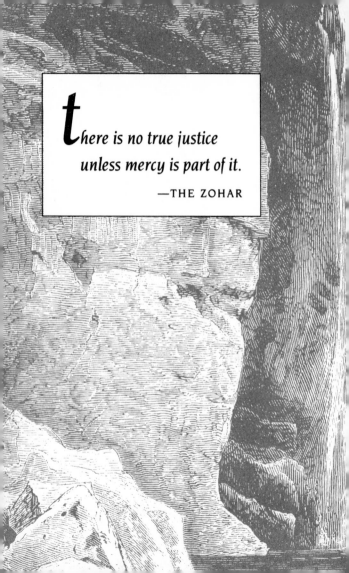

*t*here is no true justice
unless mercy is part of it.

—THE ZOHAR

*i*t is not your duty to
complete the work, but
neither are you excused
from it.

—RABBI TARFON,
TALMUD: PIRKE AVOT

*t*he best we can do to
achieve holiness is to
make a beginning and to
persevere in our efforts.

—MOSES HAYYIM LUZZATTO

a good intention is added as a good deed.

—THE ZOHAR

*t*he reward for a good deed
is another good deed. . . .

—RABBI SIMEON BEN AZZAI,
TALMUD: PIRKE AVOT

i feel that the greatest reward for doing is the opportunity to do more.

—JONAS SALK

*W*hen there is a
possibility of danger,
do not depend upon
a miracle.

—TALMUD: KIDDUSHIN

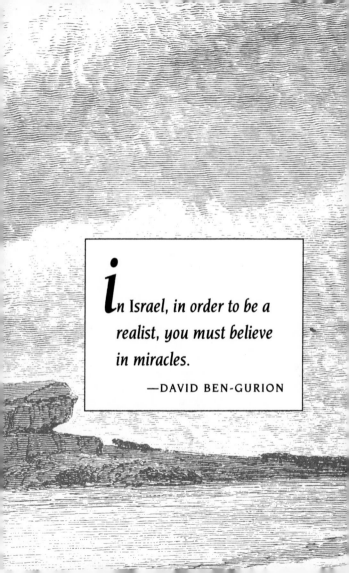

*i*n Israel, in order to be a
realist, you must believe
in miracles.

—DAVID BEN-GURION

*N*o person who is
enthusiastic about his
work has anything to
fear from life.

—SAMUEL GOLDWYN

*W*eeping may endure for
a night, but joy
cometh in the
morning.

—BIBLE, PS. 30:5

You may be disappointed if you fail, but you are doomed if you don't try.

—BEVERLY SILLS

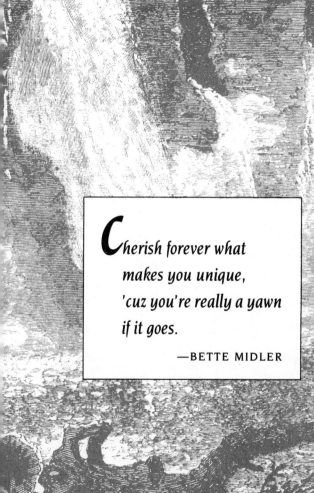

*C*herish forever what
makes you unique,
'cuz you're really a yawn
if it goes.

—BETTE MIDLER

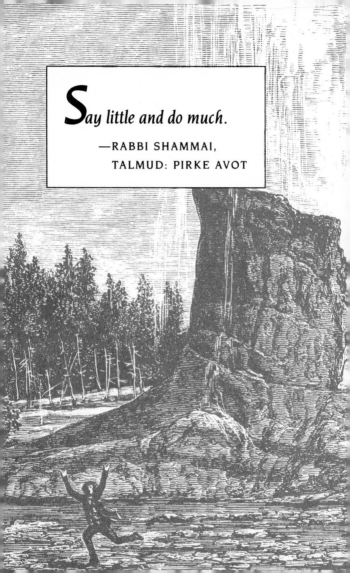

*S*ay little and do much.

—RABBI SHAMMAI,
TALMUD: PIRKE AVOT

*h*e who promises
runs in debt.

—TALMUD

*e*ven a fool, when he holds his peace, is counted wise.

—BIBLE, PROV. 17:28

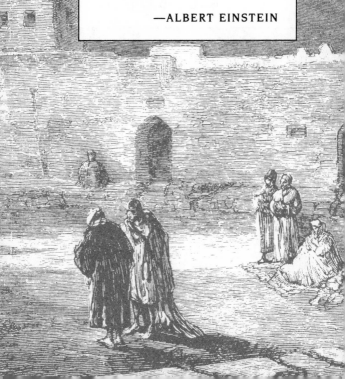

*t*ry not to become a man of success but rather a man of value.

—ALBERT EINSTEIN

*C*ompetition brings out the
best in products and the
worst in people.

—DAVID SARNOFF

*O*pportunities are usually
disguised as hard work,
so most people don't
recognize them.

—ANN LANDERS

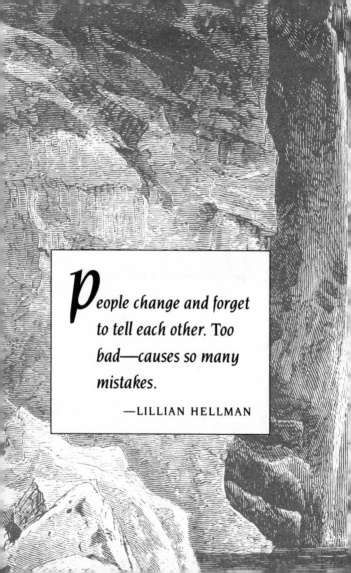

*P*eople change and forget to tell each other. Too bad—causes so many mistakes.

—LILLIAN HELLMAN

*W*hy does a woman work for ten years to change a man's habits and then complain that he's not the man she married?

—BARBRA STREISAND

*W*hether women are better than men I cannot say—but they are certainly no worse.

—GOLDA MEIR

*d*eath is not the greatest loss in life. The greatest loss is what dies inside us while we live.

—NORMAN COUSINS

*t*o everything there is a
season, and a time for
every purpose under
heaven. . . .

—BIBLE, ECCLES. 3:1

*t*hose who do not grow,
grow smaller.

—RABBI HILLEL,
TALMUD: PIRKE AVOT

*W*hat grows never
grows old.

—NOAH BENSHEA

*S*lowly we adjust, but only
if we have to.

—ELLEN GOODMAN

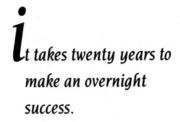

*i*t takes twenty years to
make an overnight
success.

—EDDIE CANTOR

*M*iddle age is when a man is warned to slow down by a doctor instead of a policeman.

—SIDNEY BRODY

*t*elevision has proved that
people will look at
anything rather than
each other.

—ANN LANDERS

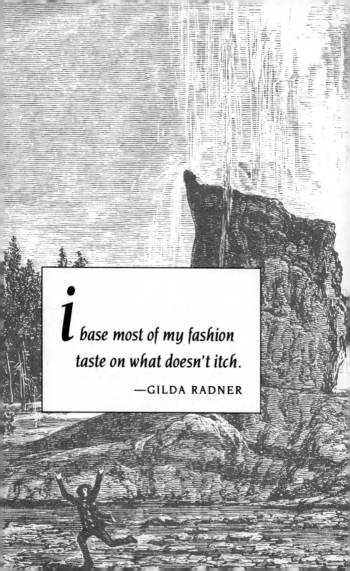

i base most of my fashion
taste on what doesn't itch.

—GILDA RADNER

*p*assions are fashions.

—CLIFTON FADIMAN

a man likes his wife to be just clever enough to comprehend his cleverness, and just stupid enough to admire it.

—ISRAEL ZANGWILL

*f*emale passion is to masculine as an epic is to an epigram.

—KARL KRAUS

*f*or every woman who makes a fool out of a man, there is another woman who makes a man out of a fool.

—SAMUEL HOFFMAN

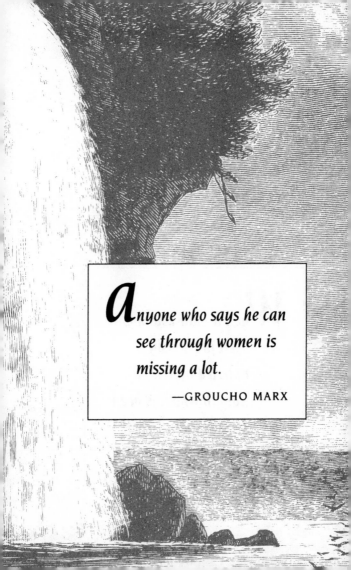

*a*nyone who says he can
see through women is
missing a lot.

—GROUCHO MARX

*W*hen a man who has been previously married marries a woman who has been previously married, four people go to bed.

—TALMUD: PESAHIM

*i*t's always something.

—GILDA RADNER

*l*ife is a negotiation.

—WENDY WASSERSTEIN

*C*ome now and let us
reason together.

—BIBLE, ISA. 1:17

*l*ust isn't all there is to sex.
Sex isn't all there is to love.
But love is almost all
there is to life.

—EDDIE CANTOR

*t*hose who can't love,
flatter.

—YIDDISH
FOLK SAYING

*O*h, what lies there are
in kisses!

—HEINRICH HEINE

*S*exual enlightenment is justified insofar as girls cannot learn too soon how children do not come into the world.

—KARL KRAUS

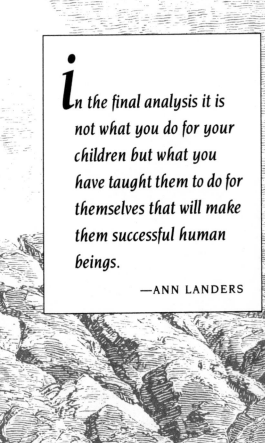

*i*n the final analysis it is not what you do for your children but what you have taught them to do for themselves that will make them successful human beings.

—ANN LANDERS

i don't want to be a pal,
I want to be a father.

—CLIFTON FADIMAN

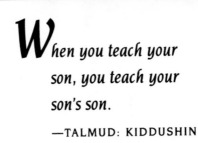

*W*hen you teach your
son, you teach your
son's son.

—TALMUD: KIDDUSHIN

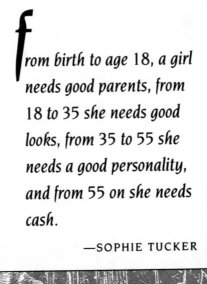

*f*rom birth to age 18, a girl
needs good parents, from
18 to 35 she needs good
looks, from 35 to 55 she
needs a good personality,
and from 55 on she needs
cash.

—SOPHIE TUCKER

*t*he reason grandparents
and grandchildren get
along so well is that they
have a common enemy.

—SAM LEVENSON

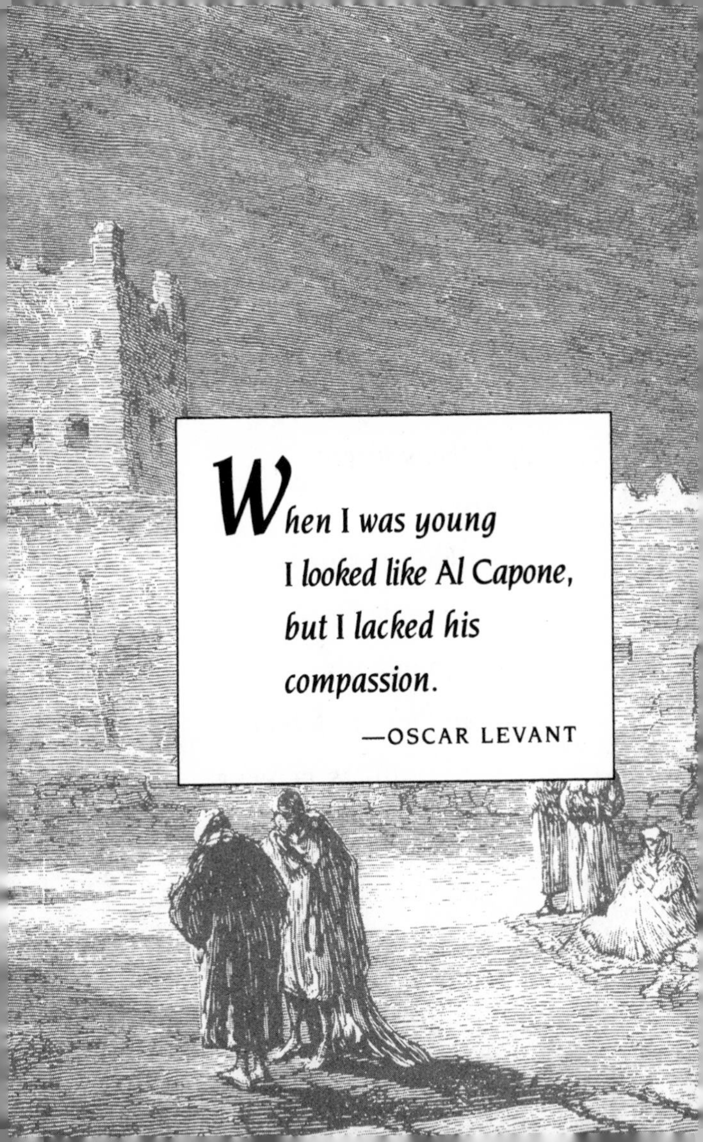

*W*hen I was young
I looked like Al Capone,
but I lacked his
compassion.

—OSCAR LEVANT

i grew up to have
my father's looks—
my father's speech
patterns—
my father's posture—
my father's walk—
and my mother's
contempt for my father.

—JULES FEIFFER

*t*he magic of first love is our ignorance that it could ever end.

—ISAAC D'ISRAELI

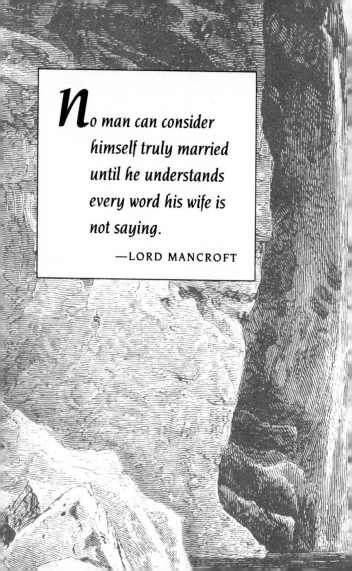

*n*o man can consider
    himself truly married
    until he understands
    every word his wife is
    not saying.

—LORD MANCROFT

*t*o be sure, the dog is loyal.
But why, on that
account, should we take
him as an example?
He is loyal to men,
not to other dogs.

—KARL KRAUS

a curse? You should have a lot of money, but you should be the only one in your family with it.

—ERNST LUBITSCH

nobody tries to steal
your troubles and
*nobody can take your
good deeds.*

—YIDDISH FOLK SAYING

*h*ow do you want your
NO, fast or slow?

—MICHAEL TODD

*t*he more charity,
the more peace.

—HILLEL THE ELDER,
TALMUD: PIRKE AVOT

M**ore people die from overeating than from undernourishment.**

—TALMUD: SHABBATH

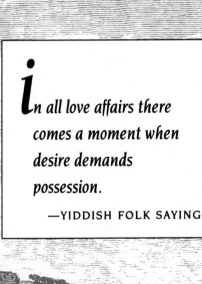

*i*n all love affairs there
comes a moment when
desire demands
possession.

—YIDDISH FOLK SAYING

*Y*ou can't push a wave onto the shore any faster than the ocean brings it in.

—SUSAN STRASBERG

*t*here must be more to life
than having everything.
—MAURICE SENDAK

*a*ll our final decisions are
made in a state of mind
that is not going to last.

—MARCEL PROUST

*t*o be old is a glorious thing
when one has not
unlearned what it means
to begin.

—MARTIN BUBER

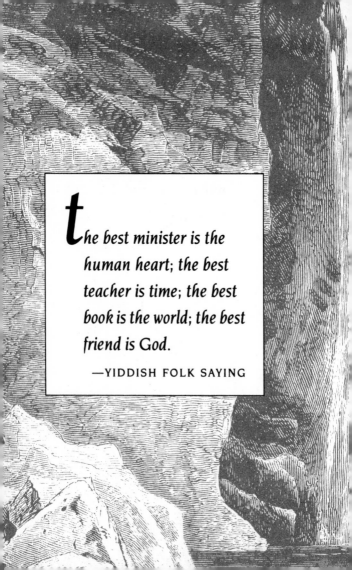

*t*he best minister is the
human heart; the best
teacher is time; the best
book is the world; the best
friend is God.

—YIDDISH FOLK SAYING

About the Author

NOAH BENSHEA is a poet, philosopher, and teacher. His international best selling JACOB THE BAKER and its sequel JACOB'S JOURNEY have been praised by theologians and scholars while his timeless insights are now told and retold by admirers around the world. Born in Toronto, Noah benShea lives with his wife and two children in Santa Barbara, California.